I0470922

Gold Investing For Beginners:

How to Invest in Gold

By

Robert Alderman

ISBN-13: 978-1490531830

Table of Contents

Gold Investing For Beginners: How to Invest in Gold

By Robert Alderman

© Copyright 2013 Robert Alderman

First Published, 2013

Printed in the United States of America

Introduction

Have you ever thought of investing in gold? Gold is one of the most stable precious metals; it is described as a protection for you and your family against financial uncertainly and inflation. This is one of the most recommended investment opportunities especially for someone who has never invested on anything before. The future for gold investments always have a golden lining since the price of the metal has increased for about three to four times its value in just a matter of a decade.

So if you have never thought of where to put your earnings to good use, invest in gold! More and more novice investors are now enjoying the reaps of their investments a decade or two ago and think of how much will gold be worth in the next ten to fifteen years? A few thousand dollars today will be worth a fortune by the time you are leaving work for retirement or when your youngest child heads to college!

Chapter 1. Why Invest in Gold

There are so many reasons why you must consider investing in gold; for one gold is gold. This is one of the most precious metals that will never be outlasted or outdated for a long time. Natural gold reserves have become harder and harder to mine and gold is becoming scarcer and scarcer; your small investment today will become a huge sum if you consider selling it.

1. Gold is global currency- wherever you live you will never need to worry when you have gold invested. At present, the US dollar is weak and some say that it may soon fall and become just another printed currency. Gold is naturally bought in US dollars and is also sold in the same currency and any decline of the US dollar also causes a decline of the value of gold. But even with this predicament, gold still holds strong and will continue to do so even when the value of the dollar becomes weaker.

2. Worldwide mining for gold is not increasing – as mentioned, our gold reserves are dwindling and most new places to look for gold are either too treacherous as in undersea gold mining or too little to be of real value like mining in forest grounds. The demand of gold on the other hand is increasing and when the supply can't meet the rising demand then the price of gold will naturally go up in the future.

3. Gold hungry countries – countries like India and China are just two of the most gold-hungry nations that just can't get enough of the metal. These countries are also increasing in wealth which means they can afford to buy more gold even how expensive it takes in the future leading to an increase in the price of gold as well.

4. Various gold trends – there are so many positive trends in gold that spell symptoms that it is a good year to invest in the metal:

a) According to experts, the last decade showed a major move for gold similar to the rise in the value of the metal in the 1970s. Gold increased in value from just $38 to $800 which is definitely a go signal for beginner and professional investors to start investing.

b) Gold funds are seen to be in the uptrend to a new market in 2012 and have continued to do so together with the bullion.

c) Gold funds on the other hand have also reached their highest values last three years ago and are still increasing to this year. Experts agree that aside from gold, gold funds are also a wise and sound investment to make.

Chapter 2. Ways to Invest in Gold

There are so many ways to invest in gold - which makes it a flexible and reliable investment. You may invest in the following when it comes to gold:

1. Gold coins – this is basically one of the most popular ways to invest in gold. You can pick the type of coin that you wish to collect. The most common are oz coins like the Canadian Maple Leaf, the American Eagle, South African Krugerrand and the Austrian Vienna Philharmonic. All these coins are not just valuable but are also prized for their beautiful quality craftsmanship. You can keep them in a secured container or you can collect then and sell them for a handsome sum. If you would like to invest in this kind of gold, be sure to learn all about the value of each and shop for the best buyer that can provide the best price.

2. Numismatic coins – these coins are much older than oz coins and are often prized collectibles or part of a historical collection. These gold coins are often appraised before they are sold. You need a huge capital to start collecting and investing in numismatic coins since these are often very expensive since you are buying a piece of history.

3. Bullions – these are gold bars that are available from as small as a gram to as heavy as 400 ounces. You can buy these precious bars from a high quality gold dealer or gold refinery; you may look for the most reputable agent online or consult your bank or trusted gold buyer or jeweller.

Selling gold bullions is easy when you also have contact with a reputable dealer. So make sure to develop a good working relationship with your gold dealer so he could help you in investing using gold bullions.

4. Gold certificates – you simply cannot hide gold anywhere or stash it anywhere with you so the best way to keep large volumes of gold is to buy gold certificates. These certificates indicate that you own gold which is in storage through a financial institution. And since you are going to rent a storage facility, there is a fee for this as well as insurance charges.

5. Options and features – These are gold contracts that are used to trade in futures exchanges. These may be used to trade or to sell short. If you choose to own gold options then you will need to follow the price of gold in the market closely to determine when are the best times to sell or to trade. If you have never traded using options then you could learn so much by talking to an investment trader to help you start with your gold investment hobby.

6. Exchange Traded Funds – ETFs are recommended as the safest way to own gold; you will buy gold shares in a fund which is priced depending on gold's market price. Aside from the safest way to invest in gold it is also the easiest to manage since you don't have to worry about storage for gold coins, bullions and priceless jewellery or insurance as well.

7. Mining certificates – gold mining certificates are proof that you own stocks of a company that mines gold. Have these stocks may be a bit hard to manage and to sell since the price of your ownership depends on the price of gold in the market but also the market value of the company or mining corporation. There are only a few companies that have become players in gold mining stocks and one of these is Market Vectors Gold Miners ETF.

8. Gold jewelry – possibly one of the most popular ways to invest in gold is to own gold jewelry. Gold is a very flexible metal and it can be made into any type of jewelry as well as combined with rare and precious stones increasing the piece's value all the more. Most beginners in investing in gold prefer to buy gold jewelry instead since it is easy to buy and are also very easy to sell. You don't need to follow a market, learn to read and follow stocks and certainly deal with brokers and analysts when you have gold jewelry.

However there are also disadvantages in owning gold jewelry. These are harder to keep since you need a safe place to store your pieces and if you have several expensive pieces you need a large vault and jewelry insurance to protect your investment. It is hard to look for pure gold as well as honest and reputable buyers. You need to ask the assistance of an experienced jeweller to help you find the best pieces to invest in. finally, if you are into antique gold jewelry which have higher value compared to traditional pieces, you need the help of an appraiser to check for the value of the piece before you purchase and of course an expert jeweller to clean and maintain the piece. But all of these set-backs are nothing compared to the value of your gold jewelry pieces should you decide to sell them in the future.

Chapter 3. The characteristics of a Good Gold Investor

They say that anyone can invest in gold, even a beginner can do it and still earn some sort of profit after several years but it takes a good gold investor to make a large profit in just a matter of a few years. Here are some of the potential characteristics of a good investor:

1. A good investor starts early. Sadly if you are looking for a huge amount in just a matter of a few years then you might as well settle for another form of trading where there are fast and large returns in just a few minutes! So if you are just starting today, then expect a huge return of your investment after ten years.

And talking about early, if you start to involve young members of your family like your teenage kids into investing and gold investing then they will have a rare opportunity to enjoy the fruits of their own labors when they start their family or by the time they retire. This is the perfect time to transform your kids into young investors who will be able to make a difference in the future.

2. A good investor studies the market. Although there are investment brokers and there is software available to use to study the market in great detail for the movement of gold, you can make a huge difference when you study the market yourself. You can become a good investor by learning the ropes of gold investment and hopefully make your own decisions to sell or buy instead of relying on professional help.

3. A good investor does not follow the flow. Because he has ample knowledge of the market for gold, he does not rely on the predictions of others and update regarding the value of gold rather he makes his own judgment and smartly does what he believes what is right. Gold is indeed increasing in value and year after year it will do but there are different market behaviors that can affect the value of the metal. You need to be optimistic and assess all the symptoms before you make a drastic action.

4. A good investor chooses the best way to invest in gold. Seeing that there are so many different ways to invest in gold, you should be able to choose the best one that will apply to your current situation. Someone who is optimistic and who loves to collect gold may choose gold coins as

well as antique gold jewelry while those who want security and a lot less hassle to keep choose stocks and gold EFT instead.

5. A good investor invests as much as 20% of his assets in gold. According to a popular television news commentator from CNBC, the ideal percentage of your assets that you must invest in gold is about 20%. But of course this is not an exact rule for everyone. If you are very much concerned about you and your family's economic future then why not invest as much as 30% but if you are just starting out and you would like a dramatic return of your investment after a decade or more then you should consider 20% as a nice round number.

6. A good investor is a smart consumer. In most cases you will need to deal with gold firms in buying or selling your gold. You will also need to deal with gold experts like jewellers and appraisers who will need to look at your gold jewelry. At any rate you will have to follow an important rule and that is to do exhaustive research on a company you are dealing with.

The best way to find the most reputable companies is through the Better Business Bureau. This is an organization that looks after consumers and record complaints and ratings of companies online and offline. There are some practical ways to look for reputable gold companies like through an investment broker, through the bank or through personal recommendations. Make sure though that you conduct a thorough research beforehand.

7. A good investor is ready for anything. He is smart and knows what's best for his family, which is why he invests in gold and all other gold investment varieties. He chooses gold over all kinds of investment to protect his family against the possible effects of deflation, troubles with the stock market and predicted currency problems in the future. So if you have these characteristics then it is best to start investing in gold as soon as you can.

Chapter 4. How Do You Buy Gold?

So now that you are certain that you would like to invest in gold, how do you begin your first purchase? Here are some tips any beginner should try out:

1. Look for the most reputable information on how to buy gold. If you choose to invest in gold coins and jewelry then an appraiser and a jeweller will be able to help you out. While investing in gold futures and funds should be addressed by a reliable broker or a brokerage.

2. It is tempting to invest as much as 20% of your assets but since you are just learning how to manage investments in gold, you may settle for 10% or lower just to test the waters. If you are buying coins however, you may go for a few thousand dollars' worth then try your luck at collecting rare and more valuable coins as time goes by.

3. In all aspects of investing in gold, you should always go for the best company that will help you improve your investment and increase your knowledge in gold investment. Your choice for the ideal firm is your key to

making it big in investment so take time to review your options correctly.

4. When you have found the company that you think will help you start in investing in gold, you may now consult a broker to help you with the best option of gold investment. A broker will help you find the best company to invest in if you are investing in gold stocks and gold mutual funds. He will also be able to help you to sell your stocks in the future.

Another work of a broker is that he may act as a manager of your account especially when you have a lot of investment to start. You may either consult him regarding the market value of gold or you may just hire him to do everything for you and just settle for a daily or regular report on your investment. In most cases, stock brokers and brokerage firms usually are paid for their work so expect to pay your broker a percentage or a specific rate depending on your contract. Again, a smart investor should always research on the best brokerage company or stock broker before entrusting your hard earned money.

5. Follow the market closely. Even when you have secured the services of a stock broker or an analyst, a beginner investor learns through experience.

Beginners need to develop confidence in their ability to predict the movement of gold in the market especially when you want to make this as a full time investment and not just a simple hobby. It is also important to review different gold trends and various factors that can affect the price of gold in the market especially when the US dollar is used for the value of gold.

Chapter 5. Gold Scams

It is very important in learning about gold investing for beginners the most common concerns in buying and selling gold: gold scams. There are so many gold scams in the market today and here are some of the most ruining scams that you may encounter as you begin to explore buying and selling gold.

1. Incorrect gold grading – how are gold coins and gold jewelry graded? Different appraisers have their own way of grading cold pieces and since beginners have no idea how this is done, they end up mostly getting less for what they have. To make sure that this won't happen to you, take time to find three or four appraisers to check on the value of your gold coins and gold bullions to be certain of the best value that you are looking for. If you are appraising jewelry then you don't need to worry. Jewellers will be happy to stand by his pieces and a third party appraiser is no problem at all.

2. The fake gold bullion – so you think the fake gold bullion stint has ended during the Wild Wild West days? Wrong? There are still fake gold traffickers these days that go around looking for beginners to con and they do not go around bringing actual fake gold bullions but fake gold certificates. All sorts of made-up stories would be told just to con beginner investors into thinking that he is buying actual gold stashes.

Another popular con gold story is about scaring people who have gold bullions or gold jewelry that it is dangerous to stash these at home. They may suggest jewelry insurance or a place where these may be placed where they could be protected and cared for. Most beginners would fall prey into these con artists since they have a way to insist that they have the most updated information.

The best solution to this problem is to have a safe and secure place to store your gold bullion and gold jewelry. There are safety deposit boxes in banks or you may purchase one yourself. And of course whatever you do, NEVER fall for someone who would like to strike a bargain or a deal with you about gold. Always do business with a reputable and experienced dealer only.

3. The Salomon Index – the Salomon Index is an annual index that shows the appreciation of gold at a rate of 12%

to 25% per year; sounds like you can get rich easily when you base your investment using this index. However this was based on a selection of 20 rare gold coins and thus may not hold true for all gold investments. Oftentimes, dishonest traders may use this index to trick beginner investments; con artists will use the Salomon Index to entice new investors to invest in gold to get rich quick.

So what to do with con artists who would like to con you out of your money using this age –old technique? Just be very realistic in your judgment of how gold investing goes. If this was the case, then no one went to business and just simply invested in gold instead! Therefore, as a beginner investor, you should learn all about gold investing and how different activities in the market can affect the value of gold.

Here are just some of the most common gold scams that you may stumble upon as you test the waters of gold investing. There are so many ways to get rich with gold investment but it takes time and a lot of patience to actually do these so you can get the best investment results after quite some time.

Chapter 6. Essential Gold investing Tips

How to win in a gold investment? Experienced gold investors will tell you to study, study and study. There are no other ways to win in any type of investment than to learn all you can in the market. Here are some important tips to get the upper hand in a gold investment:

1. Enrol in gold investment seminars and conferences – there are so many online gold investment seminars that you can attend to but be careful about choosing the most suitable company or group that will conduct seminars. There are so many con groups that are waiting for beginners like you. They may conduct seminars about how to study the market for gold and how to begin your initial investment but towards the end of the conference they would start selling books, certificates and even indulge you to buy different items that will "help" you become rich in gold easily.

2. Join online forums about investments – there are online forums meant for investors who are interested in gold. Choose sites that are intended for your country or region so that you will learn more about the trends of gold in your specific market. You will get too much help from forum members as they share their experience with gold investing; ask pertinent questions that bother you about gold and all the things that you want to learn about the market and you will be readily helped by members or forum moderators.

3. Subscribe to investment sites – there are so many online investment sites that you can subscribe to but there are only a few sites that are worthy enough to subscribe to. Choose sites that concentrates on gold investment like USA Gold; these sites provides handy information on how to start investing in gold for beginners as well as investing in silver coins. You can also regularly check their site for breaking gold news, daily market report, all about the live price of gold and all about gold trading and storage. Sites like these will not just be handy for beginners but to professional investors since it offers impressive online resources and guides to easily trade gold.

4. Talk to investment experts – take the time to talk to professional investors so you can get real tips on how it is to trade, buy or sell gold. You may also get juicy tips on how to avoid scams and how to spot the best trend in the market for buying gold.

5. Follow the market – whether you are just planning on how to trade gold or you are already into buying, selling and investing in gold you need to follow the market closely. Remember that gold is just like any investment, its value rises and falls due to factors that directly affects it day after day. You will easily get the upper hand in investing in gold if you personally study the market and make expert decision on when to trade or not.

Conclusion

Now that you know all the important things about gold investing, it's time to make the best choice that you will probably make in your life. Do you want to enjoy your retirement with your family? Do you dream of a stable future for you and your kids? Does your child plan to go to med school or law school for college? Do you fear financial uncertainty in where you live? If you answer yes to most of these questions then you need to start thinking of investing on the most lucrative investment market of all: gold investment.

With your smart investment strategy, you will be able to live the life you can only dream of and enjoy the luxuries that you and your family have always wanted to have. If you have worked all your life and have yet to enjoy the pleasures of life then you desperately need to prepare for your future. Gold investment will continue to improve and you must never overlook this great opportunity at all. Prepare for your future and make your investments count! Consider gold investing and join the many that are looking forward for the best things that life has to offer.

Thank You Page

I want to personally thank you for reading my book. I hope you found information in this book useful and I would be very grateful if you could leave your honest review about this book. I certainly want to thank you in advance for doing this.

www.ingramcontent.com/pod-product-compliance
Lightning Source LLC
Chambersburg PA
CBHW071602170526
45166CB00004B/1756